before i break—
i exhale.

a collection of poems

~

DERICK J. SCHULTZ

Copyright © 2015 Derick Schultz

All rights reserved.

ISBN: 1508532699
ISBN-13: 978-1508532699

DEDICATION

For all gay youth growing up in rural areas

CONTENTS

	FRUSTRATION, CONFUSION, PONDERANCE, ANGER	Page
1	Palpitating Beats	4
2	Very Seldom Do I Cry	5
3	You Gave Me Roses	6
4	Sweet Boy	7
5	Gun Shy	9
6	Bathroom Stall Scrawl	10
7	Bottom Line	11
8	Elevator	13
9	My Soliloquy	17
10	lbs	18
11	Silence	19
12	Wine-Stained Lips	21
13	At the Market	22
14	Upside-Down Pink Triangle	23
	BLISS, PEACE, RELIEF	
15	i exhale.	26
16	My Muse	28

17	Lips	32
18	Bowties	33
19	Uncharted	34
20	Onion Peels	35
21	Routine	36
22	Trade Off	37
23	Hot Tea	38
24	Weekly Date with MS	39
25	Clawfoot Tub	40
26	Stethoscope	41
	HEARTBREAK & GRIEF	
27	Glass Slipper	44
28	Rose Bush	45
29	My Beating Heart	47
30	Bittersweet Confection	48
31	You Said	50
32	Windowpane	52
33	Cappuccino	54
34	I Shiver	56
35	Water Stain	57

VARIOUS VERSELETS

36	Murderous Dray	62
37	Marilyn	63
38	Alanis	65
39	Positive	67
40	"Vote No"	68
41	I Dreamt Hard Last Night	71
42	Leaves	72
43	Cancer	74
44	/ife	75
45	When the Smoke Finally Clears	76
46	Matriarch	77
47	Bashful	78
48	She-Devil	80
49	My First Pride	81
50	Through These Eyes	83
51	I Will Meet My Love at a Dim-Lit Poetry Reading	84
	Letter to Self	86

FOREWORD

You could call me a compulsive poet. Sometimes in the middle of the night I half-awaken and write entire poems. Many of my favorite works are created in this half-dreaming state where the writing lacks any conscious restraint or filter. I wake up to lines I usually do not even remember writing; however, on page are truths and emotions subliminally sequestered.

*

Throughout my days I find myself scribbling lines and stanzas on scraps of paper. I tuck them away in my pant pockets for future use. My memory is terrible so more times than not I forget to empty my pockets. This results in many of these scraps "meeting their maker" in the spin cycle on laundry day. I ponder the meaning contained on these dampened pieces of paper as I attempt to make out the smeared ink. The poems printed on the pages to follow are among the survivors.

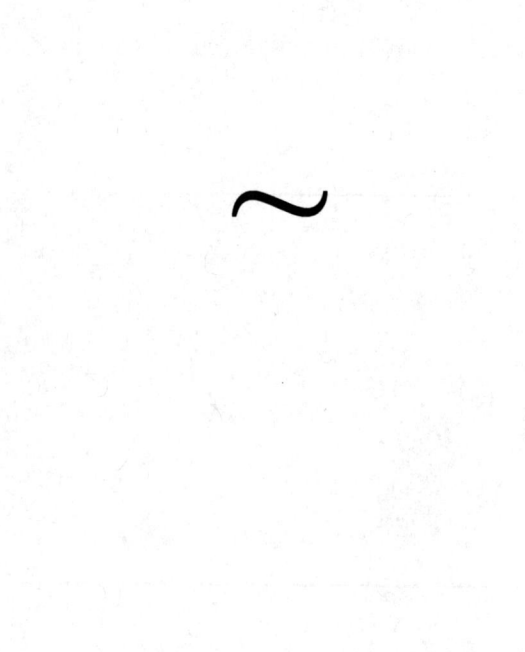

"I have the choice of being constantly active and happy or introspectively passive and sad. Or I can go mad by ricocheting in between."

-Sylvia Plath

I.
frustration, confusion,
ponderance, anger

PALPITATING BEATS

Spiraling 'round by the means

of firewater and the desires

of a subconscious mind,

I dance.

Here, at some hole-in-the-wall,

free-for-all

orgy of plaid, glitter, Gaga and hungry eyes

that feast

on my soul.

Come, come closer…

the beat in-sync with the shake

of your hips and

the tango of our tongues.

Pull me in, hold me tight,

then let me go.

VERY SELDOM DO I CRY

Very seldom do I cry.

The levees have been built so high

they lock in the water and leave

my cheeks dry.

Hands trembling in lap

I collapse.

Supposed love and lust

writes this same scene

of heartbreak and distrust.

Must I stop all this fuss

and simply love self first?

YOU GAVE ME ROSES

you gave me roses.

with teeth I tore

petal from stem.

SWEET BOY

Sweet boy,

you ask what I'm looking for?

It's really such a chore

in a city like this where boys

think they can play the one

who opts not play their game.

Shame, really

and you may regard this as silly,

but I am looking for my

gay emperor penguin.

No model mannequin or

romance from Harlequin,

just a boy that can take me

and only me,

out to din-din.

Hold me and *only* me

tight all through the night,

recede from fights and brush off all things trite.

It's a long shot.

One dot in a half-tone.

Seems like my cellular phone will never

sing, sing that ring, ring.

Instead, lingering loud

are voids at three in the morning.

GUN SHY

you ask why i am gun shy to your affection.

why i pull away from your touch,

turn cheek to your kiss,

why i shut down in quicksand conversations of love.

you ask why and i reply,

"why does a dog flinch when a hand

reaches to pet him?"

BATHROOM STALL SCRAWL

I sit toilet-seat-top in thoughts and body removed from

my sister's white gown line dancing to Cotton-Eyed Joe.

Word "fags" cut deep into bathroom stall door,

"kill all" preceding it.

I am home again to my roots—

corn fields, dirt roads and people on surface simple and kind.

I can't help but question my own fate.

Could I ever get married here without the word "fag"

being carved into *my* back?

Would faces I've known since child, turn noses up

and frowns down at my ceremony?

Same-sex.

BOTTOM LINE

I ain't an easy fuck,

no random hook-up,

so get your mind off my body

and your eyes off my ass.

This boy's got brains,

this boy's got class.

No rum on the rocks is

gonna get you in.

Whip out the pick-up lines,

tell me how I look so fine

and I'll pretend to be flattered.

You'll be thinking you got a shot,

chest puffed out,

devil-may-care grin and pout,

but truth be told

I look at you in doubt.

You'll swipe your cards

trying to impress—

body and bandages undressed—

I lose composure.

I'm still trying to get closure

from the last who left

with my heart in hand,

ripped from chest,

scars visible beneath this v-neck.

So I've heard that pick-up line

just about three dozen times,

just break through the bullshit

and get down to your bottom line.

ELEVATOR

Right index finger pushes

the elevator up button.

I stand before the sliding doors, fixated,

arm numb from the baggage weighing heavy

on my bandaged forearm

(nursed from the third degree inflicted weeks ago).

My suspense heightens as I await

the fate of the face that lies beyond the elevator doors—

most likely those of a stranger,

a stranger I will never be confronted with again.

As I wait my mind,

like a car, breaks abruptly on wet pavement—

hydroplaning off course—

who is behind that door?

As soon as I digest the question it regurgitates

and I must eat it again with

my uncoordinated chopsticks.

Among other unanswered questions like,

"Where is this elevator taking me?"

"When will it arrive?"

"How many more floors?"

"*Who* is behind the door?"

Perhaps it is my mother...

dark features and brown eyes a mirror to mine,

tears welling the night I came out—

catalyst still unknown—

yet her love has shown to be unwavering.

I hug her hard.

An exchange grown unfamiliar since childhood.

Blame it on the miles between us.

Perhaps it is my lover…

not yet discovered,

uncovered beneath the last stone turned.

He wraps his arms around my tired spine

and straightens me up—

whispering sweet somethings in my ear,

his breath hot on the skin of my earlobe,

his musk stimulating my olfactory senses.

Perhaps it is the reaper…

confronting me on my last day—

the seventh of May—

already grey at just twenty-two years of age.

I open my eyes to the cold metal doors.

The down arrow light turns cherry and is accompanied

by a delightful chime.

The doors slide open,

revealing an empty elevator car

with forgettable instrumentals and a burnt out light bulb.

MY SOLILOQUY

The utopia I inhabit, an enigma

in my mind

that dreams of the quintessential

blissful ending found on the cusp

of a tale featuring Prince Charming.

But not so charming

as he brings me a drink laced

with nepenthe.

Agroof I fall and

he catches me gallantly.

He is pompous, quixotic

and sends my heart into

a clandestine brouhaha.

I abruptly awaken from spell

once I'm hit with the gelid truth.

That he will not exist nor care

passed Saturday night,

on Sunday morning.

LBS

seat cushion sinks low

beneath my toosh.

closer to the floor i gravitate as

my knees move upward

(direction opposite of my self-image).

three (lbs) up since

my last confrontation with the scale

i stow away beneath my vanity.

how toxic.

one day i'll win this fight.

soles pressed to the cold metal,

eyes apathetic to the

numbers passing beneath

the once almighty, red needle.

SILENCE

Petal ripped by stigma,

floating in the breeze

among the grass and trees

of the open Midwestern plain.

Lashed and slashed by the verses,

silenced by the fear,

drowning in the tears

that trail his bloody face.

He's Sheparded by only the stars

casting a dull glow.

Clutching on tight,

fighting for life,

the emitted light creates

a glittered gleam in his eyes.

"Come, bring me harmony.

A world where man respect man,

human identify human—

Jimmy and Jack,

Jenny and Jane,

Johnny and June."

The silence is deafening.

When will it end?

One hand holds hand of the same,

the other a gun with shame.

WINE-STAINED LIPS

Wine-stained lips, red,

hair disheveled,

thoughts aloof,

I turn to my left.

The face not familiar,

the situation becoming more so.

Again I feel hollow,

depleted.

I am

departing from dalliances.

Come, rescue me please,

old-fashioned romantic.

AT THE MARKET

I pick through nearly three dozen apples

'fore I find one that is ripe to my eye.

It's green and slightly bruised,

but so am I.

Craving its sweet juices for months,

I sink my teeth into its skin

and hand the farmer seventy-five cents.

UPSIDE-DOWN PINK TRIANGLE

Stereotypical, ignorant, blinded by religion and tradition
you whisper, shout, stare—even glare as
I simply walk by minding my own. Where does all this originate?
Do you think I chose to be gay?
Why would I choose this?
A life filled with rejection and discrimination—
with struggles, hardships and
a constant yearning for acceptance.
Shot by the hateful words you spew
and cut by your eyes of judgment.
Am I asking too much?
All I seek is equality.
Rights that you take for granted,
I fight and have fought for.
Regardless of the
oppression
brought on by conservative agendas,
religious and political alike,
I will find my
love,
and *he* and I will
walk together
hand-in-hand,
living life
limit-
less-
ly.

"The only emotion that is bottomless for me is joy."

-Alanis Morissette

II.
bliss, peace, relief

I EXHALE.

a wet kiss on forehead

awakens me from slumber.

i could get used to this.

you tickle my sore ribs

even as i beg you to stop—

you have me giggling like a child—

i've never laughed so hard.

your heavy hands wrap around my back

and straighten my tired spine.

i exhale.

you sink your teeth into my troubles.

trembling, my emotions are apparent.

without doctorate you dive into me

ex and internally to understand

what no other does nor dares.

the mask falls off with a thud

and you do not cringe

in the face of the imperfections

that my insecure psyche kept hidden

behind the black veil—

i exhale.

MY MUSE

You say, you say…

"Hey, I don't believe we've formally met."

Salutation accompanied by a meek smile,

yet a firm handshake.

I keep my cool on the surface,

but inside I'm melting

(a fallen ice cream cone, now a puddle on an

oven-baking summer sidewalk).

I somehow conjure up a smile in response.

The nonverbal communication of your eyes,

your smile is singing a ballad

as you pluck a Forget-Me-Not from the

flower pot sitting on the windowsill

of the window looking into my room.

Through the window looking into my room,

I am vulnerable, exposed to your eyes

and smitten by your charm.

Inside you peruse the cubbyholes of my soul,

the clutter in my room,

stored and organized in cardboard boxes

stacked as high as the ceiling,

each one faced with name of lover, comma, year

in Sharpie marker.

But you aren't consumed by the clutter

as heaping as it may initially seem.

You just look at me and smile.

Smile that smile which

results in my heartbeat playing hopscotch then

Double Dutch on an abandoned playground.

You come back around,

come back around,

come back around.

Perfection is created by the eye

that sees that the imperfections are trivial and

that the big picture is the true art to be admired.

How sweet, you reserved the gallery

just for me.

Too good my dear, my love, my new found boo,

I wanna be, I wanna be, I wanna be loved by you, you,
you—

no, this isn't a sappy worn-out

proclamation, a cheesy affirmation

or boom box held above head

outside your bed

awakening you from a deep dream of rings and rainbows.

Take my hand,

take my hand so we can be one.

The feeling of our hands interlocking,

lock in key,

unlocking my bedroom window—

Cupid is stabbing me

with his arrow.

Aphrodite goes in for the win

and I let you in.

The boxes disappear,

for the past elicits no fear, no tears.

The future opens up to a whole new hope

as I'm reassured,

reassured by your smile.

"Oh please, oh please

won't you come in and stay awhile?"

LIPS

Your lips gently tug

the lower of mine,

our bodies intertwined

like a twist tie

sealing off the air to

a loaf of rye.

BOWTIES

Bowties get me hot and heavy—

makes me such a petty

gush with a school girl crush

on this geek chic treat—

"bon appetite!"

Breathe.

Delicate bow hugs Adam's apple

as he pleasurably hits that high note ♪

UNCHARTED

Come, come to me.

Keep me warm

with your company.

Shhh, don't say a word,

your eyes tell all.

No longer a free-for-all

battle of emotions.

Sans sense of

complacency,

new tenant to the

vacancy

in my heart.

Come, darling, make me feel

uncharted.

ONION PEELS

we hugged for twenty minutes

                                      in a peppermilling crowd

your arms felt so good again around

                                      my ribs

crow's-feet-stamped-eye-corners

                                      smiled deep

onion skin of a year peeled away

                                      before my watering eyes

we danced in tandem like ghosts of yesterday

                                      as peels crunched underfoot

ROUTINE

vinyl record drops into turntable.

static is followed by an all too familiar tune.

click-clacking typewriter keys meet paper

and sipping lips meet wine glass rim.

incense burn a scent of tranquility.

words, sentences, ideas

are borne into existence,

a product of this routine process.

emotions pour, unfiltered—

releasing the weight of the heavy thoughts

polluting a neurotic mind.

continuous rhythm bores serendipity.

TRADE OFF

Discombobulation paired with

a burning head of lonely—

rinse and repeat remedy—

I long for a cooling.

Ice cubed glass

pressed to neck

cools my hot flesh.

Whispers crescendo to

loud sounds and the unfound affection

I crave. I tap into a well of alcohol

frequented by short-sighted souls

with smiles and intentions deceiving.

Trading the nightclub hubbub for coffeehouse zen,

deejay record spin for cappuccino steamer squeal,

I find eyes less hungry for sex

and more appetizing to conversation and a scone.

HOT TEA

Hot tea, warm bed.

Just me and the thoughts

percolating in my head.

WEEKLY DATE WITH MS

Oversized, cord-knit sweater clad

I descend a winding stone stairwell

journal in hand,

leaves crunching under sole

afoot to the beach clearing.

Tree trunk uprooted,

planked on stump and sand

provides a seat, the beach our table.

Ducks tread ripples toward me

against your current—your greeting.

My date every Sunday, religiously,

I light a flame,

read you my poems

and you dance

with a body of waves—your reply.

CLAWFOOT TUB

Sitting crisscross applesauce

in a clawfoot tub

hot droplets splat

against skull and white porcelain—

tintinnabulation—

I breath slow.

Water fills the tub and hot steam my lungs

as my toe acts as a plug.

Warm water cuddling my bones

trumps the chill of a

widowed queen bed.

STETHOSCOPE

We sat bed center

on the verge of a kiss.

I paused, turned left and from nightstand drawer

pulled a stethoscope.

Headset to your ears

and cold, metal turntable to my heart.

A steady beat retreats,

then races rapidly

once our lips meet.

"Depression can be the sand that makes the pearl."

-Joni Mitchell

III.
grief and heartbreak

GLASS SLIPPER

prince charming places the

slipper on the wrong foot—her's—

as I stand there staring.

chin dropped & bottom lip quivering

i stumble into a pedestal.

a vase—blue—

hits the floor shattering,

mimicking that of my heart.

charming warns, "watch your step."

ROSE BUSH

The ground soil is moist

from late evening showers,

giving power to the flowers

and a salty taste on my lips.

I can hear the bees buzzing,

"honey, you left me here."

I'm at a loss, mental floss,

Mister Sandman misinterpreted

my dream and gave me nightmare.

Fair enough. How did I get here?

I remember

I danced all night on your street

in the crying rain.

Weak at the knees from the intoxication and pain,

I tumbled into a

roadside rosebush in your front yard,

its thorns like shards

cutting into flesh,

opening wounds not so fresh.

MY BEATING HEART

My hands grasp some sweet concoction

as my mind runs in circles,

my walk begins to stagger

and my vision begins to blur.

I'm taken away to some distant place

where all my worries dissipate

and my beating heart is no longer numb

from the first stab penetrated.

Your gentle hand rubs my back

as my head meets the toilet;

puking away all disgust

I have for him,

reopening my tattered heart

to let you in.

BITTERSWEET CONFECTION

The most breathtaking sound is the one

I hear when my head lays on your chest.

Your heartbeat thumps against my ear

as rain ricochets off the window glass.

This relationship we have is deep, yet discrete,

cannot be leaked or concrete,

which is hard, so hard to limit

my affections to behind locked doors

and in dark rooms where ghosts haunt

of what could be—

give taste of a confection

so sweet and decadent on tongue.

Write this recipe down

so I can serve it all day long

while playing our song, "Moon River," in record player console.

It's crackly from wear, but still preserving,

of the first night we met.

I bet we would not have guessed we'd be

where we are today.

To say that our love is patient

is an understatement.

For forty years I've had to hide my other half.

To them, you are just a friend, not my spouse,

even though we share a house—

a house in this small, conservative town

who frown upon a union of ours,

a union at its core no different than theirs.

With a sigh you reply,

"Honey, I suppose sometimes life just isn't fair."

YOU SAID

You said "I love you,"

I hesitated an echo.

So low you fell and

into the darkness you ran—

promising of no return.

It slipped through my fingers

like a thick, gooey syrup—

slow and sticky—

leaving my eyes sappy

and my hands unpleasantly

stuck to the telephone.

Ear subject to the dial tone drone,

my fingers hesitate to punch the numbers.

Clock ticks.

Why didn't I pick the apple while it was ripe?

Too trite life is now,

a surround sound of sorrow.

Regrets pile up, heaping—

dirty laundry, neglected to be washed—

mismatched sock after sock.

What now?

I know now that I,

I should have loved you presently.

Once a mainstay, now merely a poem

tucked away in these pages.

WINDOWPANE

Rain droplets fall on windowpane,

faintly I hear you call my name,

but nowhere in sight

are you, Mister Right.

I suppose I have myself to blame.

Horizontal lines through window blinds

cast light on my thinning countenance.

Shadow bars restrain me to this bed once shared,

the venue we indulged in

every fiber of each other's being.

I see you have moved forward.

In public I will reflect the same.

Yet the thought of you

echoes,

a cadence

sung in the grotto

of my pernicious soul.

CAPPUCCINO

I was hesitant,

you insisted we have coffee.

Open-minded I sipped cappuccino,

you an iced latte—

the wheels started to turn over shy smiles and small talk.

You call, "Come on up."

I follow your command.

I'm greeted with a dozen roses—

pink and white, my favorite—you listened.

I stand staring at them flattered and confused.

Intellectual intercourse reveals

both of our insecurities, dreams and interests.

I eat every bite you feed me—comfort food,

so delicious—

in haste I burn my mouth.

Suddenly the conversations change.

Exchange abruptly feels disconnected, cold.

I am reeling after your initially heavy pursuit.

Now I'm caught and you are

hung up on ghosts of past.

Meanwhile I'm left with the chore of coping.

Déjà vu story of a love addict.

I SHIVER

For three months no sun shined in.

The blinds were shut so tight

no direction pulled or yanked would release them.

A recluse in my room I sat

with blank stares and an unrelenting fear.

You said, lend me your love and I'll pay you back in kisses.

Your arms wrapped around my bones,

I shivered.

Inebriated and incoherent,

I gave no consent to

the bandit masquerading as a friend.

WATER STAIN

when you left i cried.

tears fell to the floorboards

producing a puddle.

after not being wiped dry,

a water stain

remained forever ingrained.

i cover it with a rug,

exotic and oriental.

on its fibers i ruminate and meditate—

eyes shut, mind wading deep

while incense burn—

healing the feeling of abandon.

under this rug where that stain remains

i press my veins and

my heartbeat thumps against the grain.

"I restore myself when I am alone."
-Marilyn Monroe

IV.
various verselets

A MURDEROUS DRAY

Outside my window

the crows and the squirrels play together—

one of fur, the other feathers—

despite their differences

they mingle in the Minnesota snow—

a murderous dray on this January day.

MARILYN

Her smile beams 'cross face,

ear to ear.

Sheer glamour, beauty, class,

people in mass run to see her

on the screen bigger than any found

in any living room or door.

Her breathtaking essence, ruby red-lipstick

and Chanel No. 5 her scent, so classic.

Oh, what a chore it must have been

to be so painstakingly perfect in the eyes

of all but herself.

Deep resentment for fame,

behind the million dollar smile

hidden tears remain on reserve

until the lights are dimmed, microphones muted

and cameras retired.

Clenching a rotary-dial phone

she makes one last cry of desperation,

one final plea for help;

the climatic curtain call

to her long-suffering self.

ALANIS

The spine of a compact disc case

glistening in the summer sun caught my eye

amidst dozens of others lined neatly

in a cardboard box in a stranger's driveway,

priced five dollars—the year 1999.

It read "Jagged Little Pill".

I handed the owner four bills,

three quarters, two dimes and a nickel

(excavated couch cushion coins

and allowance left over).

A beautiful explosion of anger and honesty met my ears

in the backseat of my parents' car

as I pressed play on my "non-skip" CD player.

Like nothing I'd ever heard, I sat in a trance and

I listened.

Wine, dine, 69,

intellectual intercourse,

and him telling me he'd love me until the day that he died

(even though he's still alive),

became much more relative and real fifteen years

and two copies later.

POSITIVE

Vertical line slashed through horizontal

my worst fears would be confirmed

and my life would be forever changed

as the pursed-lipped nurse looks me in the eye

and pops that "p" to begin the word

I dread to hear.

"VOTE NO"

This poem was written in response to a proposed constitutional amendment in Minnesota that would define marriage as a union between one man and one woman. On November 6th, 2012 the measure was put to a public vote. At 2:52 A.M. on November 7th, 2012, the referendum was official announced defeated with 53% of Minnesotans voting "no" (47% voting "yes"). In 2013, Minnesota would become the 12th state to legalize same-sex marriage.

I look around and what I see?

A state that could separated by parties and policies

that discriminate, intimidate and separate—

making the minorities and the oppressed

the easy target of hate.

Republican agendas only cater to the WASPs

buzzin 'round their mansions of nests,

leaving the rest without any glimmer of hope

or remote sense of pride or equality.

This November will ultimately decide the fate

of which direction this state is going.

Fear and uncertainty is definitely showing

as we deliberate which candidate to lend our support.

Divisive issues will spark debates in our families,
communities and minds.

False fronts, dirty tactics and padded, slanted campaigns

will ignite a battle of control for all to see.

May it be the way of fairness and equality

that we decidedly vote.

At least that is my hope.

That one day I can marry the person I love.

That I won't be told I'm less than by some

conservative Joe Blow who doesn't know

Jack Squat about my love or my life.

The fact I don't need a *wife* to be happy,

a husband will suit me just fine.

It's time to look to issues that matter—

why take steps backward?

It's time to fight for an equal Minnesota,

to stand up and support your gay brothers and sisters,

to speak out for love.

Don't 'cha know?

November 6th, twenty-twelve,

you need to vote "no".

I DREAMT HARD LAST NIGHT

I dreamt hard last night.

Reality and fantasy blurred into one

very vivid scene.

I dug my heels deep into a dirt road to stop

the treadmilling ground

from pushing me toward

a black hole of uncertainty.

The darkness proved to be much less

menacing once exposed

for what it was—

skyscrapers and taxi cabs

with ears and eyes less

attentive and whispering

to my every doing.

Anonymity was refreshing.

LEAVES

Lifeless saffron-hued leaves

complete the autumnal scene within

an otherwise motionless woodland.

Ambience engulfs the atmosphere

as gold rays of sun kindle the delicate petals

of a colony of aster—their centers imitating

the entity which sustains them.

Dark clouds seize the sky,

strong winds rip through the trees and underbrush—

leaves amiss, scatter about.

Fragile petals lament as they are tore from stem.

Unseen hence to the day,

once segregated leaves and petals mix.

Petal meet petal, leaf meet leaf,

leaf meet petal.

The once lifeless wood,

now fresh and stirring,

makes for a much more titillating scene.

CANCER

Do you realize, guys, I was born

just four days shy of the 23rd anniversary

of man walking on the moon?

That as a Cancer I am emotional,

a moon sign hell-bent on finding a purpose

with a foundational purpose.

In Layman's

as lonely as Joni 1971,

with the rage of Alanis 1995,

sprinkled with the fooling ennui of Bea 1988,

Emmy in hand.

Do not step on my shell, I warn.

Pinchers will pinch deep and the

moonlight'll be blinding.

/IFE

life isn't a puzzle/why are you looking for the pieces?

life is a masterpiece/sculpted/painted/created

by the artist residing it's abode—

nested in the wilderness/perched by the sea/

resting in a farmhouse outside some

one-horse/ no-name town

where sugarplums are the fairies
of Christmastime/ not the boy next-door//

"Sodom and Gomorrah!"/

the preacher decries/

he searches the parkinglot

for his rabbitfoot keychain with verse-inscribed cross
affixed/cherry-picked//

chin up/ head high/

a good time ain't no crime/bartender, bring me a fruity
drink on the rocks 'fore i diiie.

WHEN THE SMOKE FINALLY CLEARS

Pounding the final nail in my coffin,

I'll lay un-phased by

the melee occurring around me.

The world for which I loved so dear

has died.

Is this my final stop or my penultimate end?

Is this all there is or is there more?

Who could ever know?

What all can ever be known?

On second thought, turn me to dust.

Do me one final deed:

sprinkle my ashes on a dandelion puff,

then blow them in the breeze

on the back of its seeds.

MATRIARCH

All came to you for a slice of your wisdom

and a bowlful of your chicken, noodle and dumpling soup,

homemade from scratch—

raw—borne from much patience,

experience and hardship.

Many afternoons that summer spent in

your kitchen playing rummy.

You shared stories of days passed and tidbits of life truths.

I told you to write a book,

you humbly laughed.

Sequestered memories

are now warm in my mind

as I find your photograph

in my trunk of keepsakes

and you smile back at me.

BASHFUL

My dad would comb down my cowlick

every morning over the kitchen sink

while cooking Cream of Wheat, chocolate,

on the coil burner stovetop.

Bus pulled up at seven-thirty

and he'd help pull on my cowboy boots.

My sister led the way by footprint through the snow

to the yellow at the end of the gravel driveway.

Bashful with face buried in shoulder

in response to question or eye contact;

I would cover my eyes and then believe to all else

I was invisible.

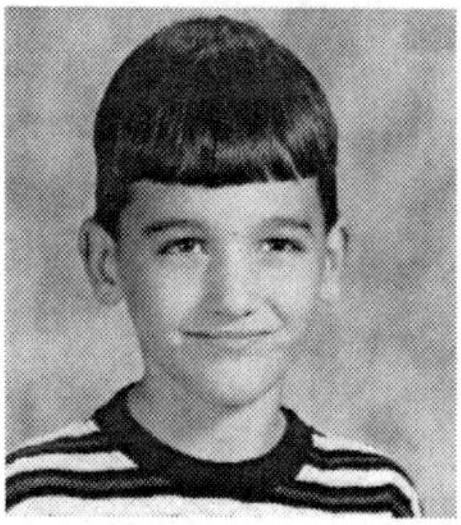

SHE-DEVIL

High-heel hooked on bottom rope

leaning in for a foot-popping kiss—

cameras flash.

Volume blonde locks and shirt cut high

reveals a tease more than midriff as

she bounces around.

Cigar puffs produce circles

outside of the squared one.

MY FIRST PRIDE

My first Pride was in June twenty-twelve.

It was then that I delved

head first into a world

that was pouring of love, acceptance and diversity.

Although temporary,

the atmosphere was refreshing.

No pack of Skittles could give me as

vivid of a taste of the rainbow

than the summer air in Minneapolis

and warm rays of sun beating down over

a village of tents pitched in Loring Park.

Music playing as people of every walk

walk on by, some flashing a smile,

others offering a word,

the rest just absorbing it all.

Not a dull moment in the next forty-eight hours,

no amount of showers could rain on this parade.

In a world all of its own,

I'm a glammed-out, glitter-doused queen on his throne.

No longer filled with the feeling of being so alone

in a secluded, conservative town

way down south and west of the met,

let this be

my hiatus from reality.

THROUGH THESE EYES

glowing embers accompanied by

crisp crackle, I sit fireside.

double old-fashioned in grasp

and unfamiliar faces in sight—

some smiling, others laughing and interacting,

the rest silent.

lips move, sip and in some instances

meet others.

divas grace mounted televisions above

and below mouths sing along verbatim.

photo flashes illuminate

many of eyes glazed,

nonetheless eager as

they look hopefully

forward to the year to come.

I WILL MEET MY LOVE AT A DIM-LIT POETRY READING

I will meet my love at a

dim-lit poetry reading.

Metal folding chair-lined rows

an audience to a single

spotlighted microphone.

Syllables released into air leave

the poet naked and bare

to front row eyes and

silhouettes that lie behind.

Crowd of pompadours and stocking caps'

fingers snap in applause.

LETTER TO SELF

dear self,

-don't let the little things get to you. do as the beatles' song suggests "let it be".

-express gratitude more often. it's okay to be vulnerable in the right situations.

-enjoy a moment in the moment. don't wait to enjoy it retroactively—it's not nearly as fulfilling.

-let your emotions be free-flowing, not stalled by any hang-ups.

-don't drink your troubles away, it only creates more.

-the quality of what you eat will translate into your mood and how you feel. eat healthier and enjoy the benefits.

-never stop moving. life is too short and too many good opportunities will pass you by.

-vent your frustrations daily. bottled up emotions are a recipe for combustion.

-never lose sight of who you are. don't compromise yourself for anything or anyone.

-focus on the moment first, love second. love will find its way to you. there is no need to search fruitlessly for it.

 -when love finds you, don't resist its calling.

-cherish and surround yourself with those that make you feel your best.

-pay no attention to the naysayers.

-be where your feet are.

and finally,

follow your dreams passionately.

-self

ACKNOWLEDGMENTS

My family for their unconditional love and support,
my dear friends for all the delicious memories and laughs
and all those—good and bad—
who inspired these writings.

ABOUT THE AUTHOR

Derick Schultz grew up on a farm outside of Tulare, South Dakota—population 207. Adolescence was not kind to a lone pansy flower growing in a field of corn stalks. He turned to writing as a means of coping and catharsis during this difficult period. In the process an insatiable passion for writing was uncovered and discovered.

Schultz currently resides in Minneapolis where most of his time is occupied working in the field of television production and writing.

CONNECT

web: percolatingpoet.com

facebook: facebook.com/percolatingpoet

electronic mail: derickschultz@hotmail.com

percolating poet

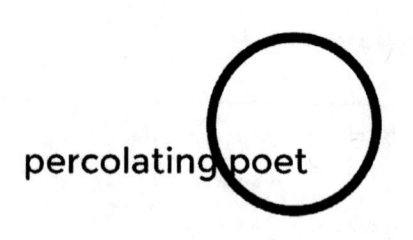

© Derick Schultz, 2015